Behind the Scenes with Charlie Heaton

The Making of a Star

Introduction

Charlie Heaton's journey from a small town in England to global stardom is one of perseverance, talent, and the courage to take chances. Many people recognize him as Jonathan Byers, the reflective and protective character from Netflix's Stranger Things. But behind the on-screen persona lies a story that resonates far beyond the glitz and glamour of Hollywood. It's the story of a young man who followed his passions, faced challenges head-on, and proved that determination can lead to extraordinary success. Born on

February 6, 1994, in Leeds, England, Charlie grew up in a working-class family. Like many small-town kids, he lived a simple life. However, a creative spark lay beneath the surface of his quiet upbringing that would later catapult him into the spotlight. From a young age, Charlie showed a knack for performance, whether through music or acting. But his path was anything but linear. In his early years, Charlie's first love wasn't acting but music. He found solace behind a drum set, playing with unbridled energy and passion. Joining the London-based band Comanechi as a drummer was his first taste of the creative world. This period in his life wasn't glamorous, but it was formative. Touring with the band and performing in small venues gave Charlie a sense of purpose and discipline. It taught him the value of hard work, the thrill of creative expression, and the resilience needed to chase a dream. Despite his love for music, Charlie's career took a surprising turn when he decided to explore acting. Without formal training or a clear roadmap, he moved to London and began auditioning for roles. For Charlie, acting was another way to express himself—to tell stories and connect with people on a deeper level. It was an entirely new world, but he embraced the challenge with the same determination that had driven his music career. What sets Charlie Heaton apart is his ability to channel his life experiences into his craft. When he stepped into the role of Jonathan Byers in Stranger Things, he brought authenticity to the character. Jonathan's quiet strength and vulnerability mirrored Charlie's journey, making his portrayal relatable to audiences worldwide. It wasn't just a role but a reflection of his life—his struggles, hopes, and resilience. Charlie's story matters because it's one in which many people can see themselves. He wasn't born into privilege, nor was his path easily paved. He faced setbacks and uncertainties, yet never let those moments define him. Instead, he used them as fuel to push forward. His rise to fame serves as a reminder that success isn't reserved for those with perfect circumstances. It's for those who dare to dream, work hard, and take risks. In today's world, where overnight success often seems like the norm, Charlie's journey is a refreshing narrative. It's a story of growth—discovering new talents, embracing change, and finding strength in vulnerability. It's about knowing that failure isn't the end but a stepping stone to something greater. Beyond his career, Charlie has become an inspiring figure for fans. His humility, grounded nature, and dedication to his craft make him relatable despite his fame. He stays true to his roots, valuing his family, friends, and passions outside the spotlight. Whether it's his love for music, his thoughtful approach to acting, or his ability to navigate the pressures of fame, Charlie's life is a masterclass in balance and authenticity. As we dive into the chapters of Charlie Heaton's life, we'll uncover the moments that shaped him into who he is today. From his early days in Leeds to his unexpected journey into acting and the monumental success of Stranger Things, each step of his story is filled with lessons and inspiration. Charlie's rise isn't just about fame—it's about finding your voice, staying true to yourself, and pursuing your passions no matter where they lead. His journey reminds us that the road to success is rarely straight, but the twists and turns make it worthwhile. Through this book, you'll discover the man behind the fame: Charlie Heaton, a rising star whose story proves that dreams, combined with grit and determination, can lead to incredible places. His tale is one to admire and learn from, making it a story that truly matters.

Chapter 1: Early Days in Leeds

Childhood Roots and Family Life

Charlie Heaton was born on February 6, 1994, in Leeds, a city in the heart of England. Leeds is known for its industrial history and bustling city life, but it was simply home for Charlie. He grew up in a working-class family, surrounded by love and support. His upbringing wasn't extravagant, but it was filled with the warmth of a close-knit family and the values that would later guide him on his journey to success. From an early age, Charlie showed a curious and creative side. He loved to explore his surroundings, often wandering through the streets of his neighborhood with a sense of adventure. While his family wasn't wealthy, they provided Charlie with the foundation he needed to dream big. His parents taught him the importance of hard work and staying humble—lessons that would stick with him throughout his life. Charlie shared a strong bond with his family, particularly his mother. She was essential to his upbringing, always encouraging him to pursue his passions, no matter where they might lead. She believed in him and his potential, even when the path wasn't clear. Her unwavering support gave Charlie the confidence to explore his interests and embrace new opportunities as they came along. The Heaton household was filled with simple joys. Charlie often played with his siblings and friends, finding creative ways to have fun without needing expensive toys or gadgets. Whether kicking a soccer ball in the park or watching movies at home, these moments shaped Charlie's early years and gave him a sense of community and belonging. Growing up in Leeds wasn't always easy. Like many families in working-class neighborhoods, Charlie's family faced challenges, especially regarding finances. But instead of letting those struggles bring them down, they used them as a source of strength. These experiences taught Charlie resilience and the importance of maximizing what you have. School was another important part of Charlie's childhood. He attended local schools in Leeds, where he was known as a quiet but thoughtful student. While academics didn't always capture his attention, he excelled in creative subjects like music and art. These classes allowed him to express himself in natural and fulfilling ways. Teachers noticed his talent and often encouraged him to explore his creative side further. Leeds itself played a significant role in shaping Charlie's personality. The city's mix of urban life and cultural heritage exposed him to diverse ideas and experiences. He often found inspiration in the everyday life around him—the people, the stories, and the energy of his community. This sense of connection to his hometown stayed with him, even as he moved on to larger cities and opportunities. As Charlie grew older, his interests began to take shape. Music, in particular, became a major part of his life. While he hadn't picked up the drums, he loved listening to different genres and imagining himself as part of a band. Music was more than just a hobby for Charlie—it was a way to express himself and find his voice in the world. Family gatherings were another source of joy for Charlie. Holidays and celebrations brought everyone together, filling their home with laughter and shared memories. These occasions reminded him of the importance of staying connected to the people who matter most. Charlie knew that his family would always be his anchor, whatever life took him. Despite the challenges and uncertainties of growing up in a working-class environment, Charlie's childhood was filled with moments that prepared him for the future. His family's love and guidance, combined with the vibrant backdrop of Leeds, gave him the tools he needed to dream big and work hard. In many ways, Charlie's early years were a perfect example of how humble beginnings can lead to extraordinary outcomes. His story shows that success isn't determined by where you start but by how you use your opportunities. Leeds may have been just one chapter in Charlie's life, but it was an important one that laid the groundwork for everything to come. Looking back on his childhood, it's clear that Charlie's roots in Leeds played a critical role in shaping his character. The lessons he learned during those formative years stayed with him as he moved into the world of music and, later, acting. His ability to stay grounded, even in the face of fame, can be traced back to the values instilled in him during his early days in Leeds.

A Young Dreamer in a Small Town

Growing up in Leeds, Charlie Heaton's childhood was a blend of simplicity and ambition, shaped by the environment of a city full of life yet far from glamorous. Leeds wasn't a place that shouted for attention; it was a city grounded in history, where working-class families made a living and carried on traditions. But for young Charlie, it was a place of possibility, a backdrop to the dreams that would one day take him beyond its familiar streets. Charlie wasn't like many other kids in his neighborhood as a child. While his friends were content with the usual pastimes of soccer, video games, and schoolyard banter, Charlie had a spark of something more. He spent hours imagining what life could be like beyond Leeds, daydreaming of adventures that stretched far beyond the horizon of his small town. Whether through the lens of music, movies, or the thought of traveling to faraway places, Charlie always sensed that there was more out there for him, waiting to be discovered. Though his family wasn't wealthy, they gave him everything that mattered—a home filled with love, support, and encouragement. His parents ensured that Charlie knew he could achieve anything he set his mind to, even if the odds were stacked against him. This unwavering belief in his potential began to fuel the young dreamer inside Charlie. From a young age, Charlie showed an interest in the arts, even though there wasn't always the financial means to pursue them. His mother noticed this early on and always tried to nurture his creative side, even if it meant finding unconventional ways to let him express himself. They couldn't always afford formal lessons in music or acting, but Charlie's love for these art forms was unmistakable. He would spend hours in his room listening to music, mimicking drummers from his favorite bands, and pretending to be on stage in front of an imaginary crowd. In those quiet moments, Charlie didn't just dream; he practiced. He believed that if he could keep pushing himself, maybe, just maybe, he could make those dreams come true. At this point, Charlie didn't have the professional tools or the means to attend acting or music schools, but he had the raw determination to make something out of nothing. He spent hours practicing drumming on makeshift instruments or performing small skits in front of his family, who always showed immense pride and encouragement despite their limited resources. It wasn't long before Charlie began looking beyond his small town for bigger opportunities. He knew that to follow his passions truly, he would need to step out of his comfort zone and venture into the world. This idea of breaking free from his small-town existence wasn't just a desire for fame or fortune; it was a yearning for growth, for expanding his understanding of who he could be. The move to London became a pivotal moment in Charlie's life. At just sixteen years old, he left Leeds behind and set off for the bustling city, carrying only a suitcase of dreams. London was the complete opposite of his quiet, small-town life. The bright lights, the fast-paced lifestyle, and the endless opportunities felt like a world he had only ever imagined. But it was here that Charlie's raw determination would begin to take shape in a way that would eventually lead to the life he had always dreamed of. While living in London, Charlie started making a name for himself by pursuing music. He became the drummer for a local band called Comanechi, a move that introduced him to the underground music scene in the city. Music had always been his first love, and performing in a band gave him a sense of purpose, allowing him to live out some of the dreams he had as a young boy. But even as he pursued music, something about acting continued calling to him, lingering in his mind. During his time in London, Charlie began to take acting more seriously. He knew it wasn't going to be easy. He didn't have formal training, and he had no connections in the entertainment world. But Charlie's belief in his ability to overcome obstacles was unshakable. He enrolled in acting classes, attended auditions, and gave everything he had to learn the craft. It wasn't long before his dedication paid off. Charlie's journey as a young dreamer from a small town to a big city wasn't without its struggles. There were plenty of moments when it seemed his dreams might slip away—times when he doubted himself or wondered if his ambitions were too big. But each time Charlie encountered a setback, he reminded himself of where he had come from and why he had started. His roots in Leeds kept him grounded and motivated him to keep pushing forward.

Chapter 2: Drumming to a Different Beat

The Journey into Music

Charlie Heaton's love for music was evident from an early age. Growing up in the industrial city of Leeds, where creativity was often a rare escape from everyday life, music became Charlie's way of expressing himself and dreaming beyond the ordinary. The beat of the drums and the rhythm pulse captured his imagination and set him on a path that would one day lead to great things. But his journey into music was not an immediate success—it was a slow, steady climb built on passion, dedication, and a belief that anything was possible. From his earliest memories, Charlie was drawn to sounds. He wasn't particularly interested in the traditional toys or games that other children enjoyed. Instead, he found comfort and joy in the rhythm of life—the tapping of fingers on tabletops, the clattering of dishes in the kitchen, the hum of the city. Something about the sound of life intrigued him, something that made him feel alive. But his discovery of the drums sparked his deep connection to music. It all started when Charlie was just a boy, no older than ten. Though not wealthy, his parents always found ways to support his interests. One Christmas, his mother surprised him with a small drum kit. It wasn't anything fancy, just a basic set of drums, but it was a gift that changed everything for Charlie. The moment his fingers struck the drumheads, a sense of excitement surged. It was as if a part of him had been awakened, and he could finally express himself in a way words alone could never capture. The drumbeat resonated deeply with him, providing a universal language that harmonized with his youthful spirit. Though Charlie had no formal training, he had an instinct for the drums. It was as if he had been born with the rhythm in his blood. He spent hours alone in his room, practicing on his small kit, hitting the drums in different patterns, and exploring sound possibilities. The act of drumming gave Charlie a sense of freedom. He could lose himself in the music, shutting out the world and playing. During these moments, he started to build the confidence he would need to pursue his passion. However, as much as Charlie loved drumming, he knew talent alone wasn't enough to make it in the music world. He needed to grow, learn, and challenge himself to improve. So, he sought other drummers and musicians who could offer him guidance and inspiration. He watched local bands, soaking in every beat and rhythm, noting how the drummers played and what made their performances special. He knew that the more he exposed himself to different styles and techniques, the better he would become. Charlie's dedication to drumming didn't go unnoticed. By his teenage years, he had become skilled enough to play in local bands. His first taste of performing came when he joined a small band in Leeds, a group of like-minded young musicians who shared his love for alternative and punk rock music. They weren't famous and didn't have much of a following, but to Charlie, it was everything. He was part of something bigger than himself for the first time—creating music with others who shared his passion. This experience opened Charlie's eyes to the world of live performances and ignited a fire in him. He loved the energy of being on stage, the excitement of playing for an audience, and the sense of connection that came with creating music in front of people. The more he played, the more he realized that music was his true calling. It wasn't just something he enjoyed in his spare time—it was the thing that made him feel alive. But the journey wasn't without its challenges. Like many young musicians, Charlie struggled to make it in a competitive and often harsh industry. The band had its fair share of struggles, from finding gigs to dealing with internal conflicts. Despite the setbacks, Charlie remained focused on what mattered most—his love for music. He knew that the road to success would be long and difficult, but he was determined to keep going. As Charlie's skills as a drummer grew, so did his understanding of music. He began experimenting with different sounds and genres, exploring everything from rock to electronic music. The more he played, the more his creativity flourished. He realized that drumming wasn't just about following a beat—it was about expressing emotions, telling a story, and creating something that could resonate with others. It was about feeling the music deep within and translating that feeling into rhythm. It wasn't long before Charlie caught the attention of the London music scene. In his early twenties, he moved to London, a city known for its thriving music culture. There, he joined a band called Comanechi, which played a blend of punk rock and experimental music. It was a pivotal moment in Charlie's musical journey. London's underground music scene opened his eyes to a new world of opportunities, and he quickly adapted to the fast-paced, ever-changing environment. The band's raw energy and unique sound helped Charlie sharpen his skills and gain recognition in music. But even as his music career began to take off, Charlie knew there was more for him. Music had always been a passion, but another form of creative expression called to him—acting. This new passion would lead him down a different path, eventually making him a household name.

Life with Comanechi

Joining the band Comanechi was a transformative moment for Charlie Heaton, marking a new chapter in his musical journey. Here, within the raw energy of punk rock, Charlie's drumming skills were pushed to new limits, and he began to truly understand what it meant to be a part of something bigger than himself. Though Comanechi was still a relatively unknown band in the bustling London music scene, the experience would shape Charlie in ways he couldn't have imagined. Comanechi was far from the polished, commercial bands that dominated the mainstream. Their sound was gritty, experimental, and loud—a fusion of punk rock, noise, and a touch of chaos. It was the kind of music that didn't follow the rules, and that's exactly what drew Charlie to the band. For a young musician like him, Comanechi represented freedom. It was a place where Charlie could express himself fully without worrying about fitting into any established mold. The band's music was driven by pure emotion, a reflection of the rebellious spirit of punk rock, and Charlie loved being a part of that creative energy. The dynamic within Comanechi was intense. Every practice, every performance, was an exercise in unleashing raw passion. The band members were fully committed to their sound and brought everything they had to each performance. For Charlie, it was an exciting yet challenging environment. He quickly realized that being a drummer in Comanechi was about more than just keeping time—it was about adding layers of complexity to the music. His drumming had to match the band's intense pace, and every beat had to carry the emotion of the lyrics and the energy of the crowd. It wasn't about playing perfectly; it was about playing with heart. Life with Comanechi also meant constant touring. Charlie and the band played gigs at venues across London and the UK, traveling from one small club to the next, meeting new fans, and encountering all the highs and lows of being in an indie band. The band's performances were far from predictable. Charlie could feel the electricity in the air with every show—the audience was as much a part of the experience as the musicians themselves. Each gig brought a new wave of excitement, a chance to connect with people who resonated with their music. But there were challenges, too. The band often faced the harsh realities of life on the road—sleepless nights, cramped van rides, and uncertain finances.

Yet through it all, the band members remained united in their mission: to make real, unfiltered, and unashamed music. Charlie thrived in this environment. His drumming grew sharper and more experimental, shaped by the unpredictable nature of the band's performances. There was no script, no set formula. Instead, Charlie was encouraged to take risks, to let the music guide him. Whether it was in the middle of a fast-paced song or a slow, brooding piece, Charlie had to stay alert, ready to adjust and adapt to whatever direction the music took. The unpredictability of Comanechi's music allowed him to push his limits and grow as a drummer. The experience also allowed Charlie to form close bonds with his bandmates. Trust and camaraderie were essential in an environment where the stakes were always high. The band's members supported each other through every rough patch, from stressful rehearsals to the grind of endless gigs. It was a unique experience that helped Charlie learn the importance of collaboration in music. He discovered that making great music wasn't just about individual talent—it was about the chemistry between musicians and how they interacted on stage and in the studio. Comanechi's music wasn't just about noise—it was about expression. Their music was designed to evoke emotions, from anger and frustration to joy and freedom. The rawness of their sound meant that every performance was an opportunity for Charlie to connect with the audience on a deep, emotional level. The louder they played, the more the audience seemed to respond, and Charlie could feel that connection every time he hit the drums. This was a new side of music for him—one about feeling as much as it was about playing. Despite their efforts, Comanechi never achieved mainstream success, but the band's impact on Charlie's life was undeniable. Their music gave him a platform to grow, experiment, and find his voice as a musician. Through Comanechi, Charlie learned not only about drumming but also about the power of creativity, the importance of pushing boundaries, and the necessity of taking risks. It wasn't about fame or fortune—it was about authenticity and staying true to the music, no matter what. Living with Comanechi also taught Charlie valuable lessons in resilience. Being in a small indie band meant facing rejection, low pay, and difficult working conditions, but

Charlie embraced those challenges because he knew they were part of the journey. Each setback was an opportunity to grow, to refine his skills, and to deepen his love for music. The band's perseverance, despite their obstacles, was something that Charlie carried with him throughout his life, teaching him that success wasn't always about immediate recognition—it was about sticking with something you believe in, even when it seems impossible. As time passed, Charlie's experience with Comanechi helped him become a more versatile and confident musician. He wasn't just playing the drums—he was telling stories through rhythm, finding new ways to express himself in every song. His time with the band, though filled with challenges, was an essential part of his musical evolution, and it gave him the foundation to pursue bigger opportunities in the future.

Chapter 3: The Leap into Acting

Finding a New Passion

Charlie Heaton's journey into acting wasn't a decision made overnight. It wasn't something he had planned for as a child or a dream he had nurtured since the beginning. Instead, it was a natural evolution of his life—a leap into the unknown, driven by curiosity and the desire to explore new creative horizons. His rise to fame through acting was a combination of opportunity, determination, and the discovery of a new passion that he hadn't initially recognized in himself. Charlie had been immersed in music for years, first as a drummer in Comanechi and later with various other projects. His love for music had defined much of his early life, and he had devoted a significant part of his youth to perfecting his craft. Yet, as time passed, he felt something was missing. He realized that while he was passionate about his music, there was a desire to do something different, something that pushed him in new directions. Music was still a huge part of who he was, but his heart longed for more—the chance to tell stories differently. That's when acting caught his attention. It all began when Charlie lived in London, a city bursting with creative energy and opportunities. While living there, he found himself in a vibrant, artistic community filled with actors, musicians, and other creatives exploring their passions uniquely. It was a city that inspired creativity, and it wasn't long before Charlie started to find himself drawn to film and television. He attended plays, watched movies, and spent time with friends involved in acting. The more he saw, the more intrigued he became by the craft. At first, acting seemed like a distant dream. It wasn't something he had ever truly considered for himself. Yet, as he immersed himself more in the film world, Charlie realized that acting offered a new way for him to express himself. It was a form of creativity beyond music—a way to step into different characters, explore new perspectives, and bring stories to life. The idea of inhabiting a character, of telling a story through performance, sparked something in him. Charlie began to realize that acting was not so different from playing music. Both required a deep understanding of emotion, timing, and connection. Just like music, acting had the power to move people, to make them feel something deep within their hearts. Charlie wasn't someone who shied away from challenges, and he knew that pursuing acting would require him to step out of his comfort zone. Acting didn't come naturally to him in the same way that drumming had. It was a different kind of expression, one that demanded vulnerability, discipline, and dedication. But

Charlie felt ready to leap. He decided to give acting a shot and began attending acting classes, eager to learn the craft and discover whether it was something he could truly pursue. At first, the world of acting was intimidating. It was a much different environment than the music scene he had grown accustomed to. Music focused on performance, rhythm, and sound; in acting, it was about transformation, understanding character, and creating believable stories. Yet Charlie quickly discovered that his background in music gave him an edge. As a drummer, he had learned the importance of timing, the ability to read a room, and the art of collaboration—skills that were also essential in acting. He realized that many of the qualities he had developed as a musician were transferable to acting, giving him the confidence to keep pushing forward. One of the most important things Charlie learned during this early period was that acting was not just about memorizing lines or following a script. It was about understanding the story and the character he was playing. He had to put himself in someone else's shoes, see the world through their eyes, and express emotions that weren't his own. It was challenging, but it was also incredibly rewarding. Each time he stepped into a new role, Charlie felt he was uncovering a different aspect of himself—one he hadn't known existed before. His breakthrough into acting came when he landed a role in the Netflix series Stranger Things, a show that would change his life forever. Charlie's character, Jonathan Byers, was a quiet, introspective teenager who played a key role in the show's mysterious and supernatural events. The role perfectly fit Charlie's talents, allowing him to explore a range of emotions and bring depth to a character that was very different from himself. The show's success helped propel Charlie into the spotlight, and it wasn't long before he became a recognizable face in the acting world. Landing the role in Stranger Things was a pivotal moment for Charlie, validating his decision to explore acting. It proved he had what it took to succeed in this new field, even though it was initially unfamiliar. But Charlie didn't rest on his laurels. He continued to work hard, taking on new roles and expanding his range as an actor. He knew the journey was beginning, and there was much more to learn and discover. Through his acting career, Charlie has continued embracing his journey's newness.

The shift from music to acting wasn't easy, but it was exactly what he needed to find a new passion. He had always loved creative expression, and acting allowed him to explore his creativity in ways he never thought possible. Over time, he found that acting was more than just a new hobby or a passing interest—it was a career that allowed him to grow as a person and performer.

Early Roles and Challenges

After Charlie Heaton decided to transition from music to acting, he faced an entirely new set of challenges. Entering the world of acting was not easy, and the road to success was far from smooth. While Charlie had the passion and determination to pursue this new path, he quickly learned that acting required more than just enthusiasm—it required hard work, perseverance, and a willingness to face rejection. His journey in acting began with smaller roles, each a stepping stone that brought him closer to his dream of becoming a successful actor. But these early roles were only sometimes easy to come by. Like many aspiring actors, Charlie had to deal with the harsh reality of auditions, where the competition was fierce, and the chances of landing a role were slim. For many actors, these early years were full of rejection and uncertainty, and Charlie was no different. Despite these setbacks, Charlie was determined to push forward. He knew each audition was a learning experience, a chance to hone his craft and grow as an actor. He spent hours preparing for auditions, studying scripts, and perfecting his performances. He understood that rejection wasn't personal but just part of the process. This mindset helped him stay focused and motivated, even during the toughest moments. He also leaned on the support of his family and friends, who encouraged him to keep going and reminded him of his talent and potential. Charlie's first significant break came when he landed a role in the British TV series Vigil. In this thrilling drama, he played a supporting character, which revolved around a submarine mystery in the British Navy. The role was a great introduction to the world of television acting, and Charlie was able to showcase his skills more substantially. Although his role was not the leading part, it allowed him to demonstrate his acting ability and gain experience working on a professional set.

Though Charlie was still relatively unknown, his performance in Vigil caught the attention of casting directors and other industry professionals. This was an important moment in his career—it proved that he had the talent to succeed in acting and could handle the demands of a professional set. However, Charlie knew this was only the beginning and that he would need to continue working hard to land bigger roles and take his career to the next level. Charlie's breakthrough moment came when he was cast as Jonathan Byers in Stranger Things, a role that would catapult him to international fame. But before that, he continued to face challenges, and the journey was far from easy. Stranger Things was a massive project; landing a role on such a popular show was a huge opportunity for Charlie. However, his success did not come without struggles along the way. In the early stages of his career, Charlie often played characters similar to his personality—quiet, reflective, and a little bit mysterious. These roles allowed him to draw from his experiences but also presented challenges. Charlie had to learn to step into different roles and transform into characters vastly different from himself. This was not an easy task, and it took time for him to find his footing as an actor. It wasn't just about remembering lines or hitting marks on the stage—it was about understanding the character's motivations, feelings, and background and bringing those elements to life in a believable way. One of the challenges Charlie faced early on in his acting career was adjusting to the pace and demands of a professional film or TV set. Unlike the world of music, where rehearsals and performances were often done in front of an audience, acting required an entirely different type of preparation. Filming could take hours, sometimes even days, and it was a test of patience and endurance. Charlie had to learn to manage his time effectively, stay focused on the task, and maintain his energy throughout long shooting days. It was exhausting, but it was all part of the job. In addition to the challenges on set, Charlie had to deal with the pressure of being in the public eye. Once Stranger Things became a global hit, Charlie's life changed dramatically. He went from being an up-and-coming actor to being thrust into the spotlight, with fans, media, and paparazzi all keen to know more about him. This newfound attention was exciting, but it also came with its own set of challenges. The pressure to perform, to live up to expectations, and to maintain a certain image in the public eye could be overwhelming. For a young actor like Charlie, navigating this pressure was a delicate balancing act. Charlie had to remain grounded and focused on his craft throughout this period. He worked hard to improve his acting skills, learning from his experiences and feedback from directors and colleagues. The challenges of early roles and the growing pressure of fame only fueled his desire to improve and prove himself as a serious actor. He understood that the road to success was long and that every role—no matter how big or small—was an opportunity to learn and grow. Early in his acting career, his struggles taught Charlie valuable lessons about resilience, determination, and perseverance. He learned to embrace rejection as part of the process, knowing that every "no" brought him one step closer to a "yes." These early challenges helped shape Charlie into the actor he is today—someone who is not afraid to take risks, step into new roles, and push the boundaries of his craft.

Chapter 4: Breaking Out with Stranger Things

Landing the Role of Jonathan Byers

After years of auditions, small roles, and struggling to make his mark in the acting world, Charlie Heaton's big break came with the role of Jonathan Byers on the hit Netflix show Stranger Things. This opportunity marked a turning point in his career, changing his life forever. Landing the role of Jonathan Byers was not only a dream come true for Charlie but also the moment that thrust him into the global spotlight. Before Stranger Things, Charlie was still relatively unknown, working through smaller roles in TV shows and movies. Although he had talent, it often felt like the big opportunities needed to be within reach. He knew that acting required patience and persistence and was ready to keep working hard. However, when the casting call for Stranger Things came around, Charlie didn't realize that this role would be the one to set him on the path to stardom. Jonathan Byers, the character Charlie would eventually play, was not a typical hero. He was quiet, introverted, and a little misunderstood. Jonathan was the older brother of Will Byers, a boy who had mysteriously disappeared in the small town of Hawkins, Indiana. Jonathan's character is deeply caring, especially when it comes to his younger brother. He was a photographer with a keen eye for capturing the world around him, but he also had a strong protective instinct, especially towards Will and his friends. Jonathan's personality was a bit of an outsider, but he was smart and had a good heart—traits that would eventually endear him to Stranger Things fans. When Charlie first heard about the role of Jonathan Byers, he was immediately drawn to the character's depth. Jonathan was not your typical "cool" character—he was real, flawed, and relatable. Charlie saw a lot of himself in Jonathan and felt that this role was something he could connect with. He knew he had the chance to portray a character with real emotional depth, a challenge he was excited to take on. The audition process for Stranger Things was intense. Thousands of actors auditioned for roles on the show, and competition was fierce. Like many other actors, Charlie had to go through several rounds of auditions. At first, he was nervous. It was a big opportunity, and he knew how important it was to perform best. He went into the audition clearly, understanding who Jonathan was and what made him unique. However, Charlie also had to make the character his own, bringing his personality and emotions to the role. He was determined to make Jonathan Byers someone special who stood out to the casting directors. During his auditions, Charlie made a strong impression. He captured the essence of Jonathan's quiet nature and his determination to protect his family. Charlie's ability to bring authenticity to the character was clear, and the casting directors noticed it. It was clear that Charlie had the potential to bring Jonathan to life in a way that would resonate with audiences. After what felt like a long waiting period, Charlie received the news that he had landed the role of Jonathan Byers. For Charlie, getting the role of Jonathan Byers felt like a huge victory. It wasn't just about landing the role—it was about proving to himself that all the hard work and years of struggling had paid off. It was a validation of his talent and dedication. But even as he celebrated, Charlie knew landing the role was just the beginning. Now, he had to bring Jonathan to life in a way that would be believable, authentic, and engaging for viewers. The next step was to dive deep into the character. Charlie spent hours studying the scripts and understanding Jonathan's motivations. He knew that Jonathan's character wasn't just about being a good brother or friend—he was a complex person with his fears, desires, and dreams. Charlie had to find a way to tap into those emotions and portray them on screen. He worked closely with the directors and the rest of the cast to understand Jonathan's relationship with his family, especially with his brother Will, and how Jonathan navigated his role in the story. Jonathan's quiet strength was one of the most important aspects of his character. While other characters in Stranger Things were loud and adventurous, Jonathan was more reflective and thoughtful. He deeply loved his family and would do anything to protect them, even if it meant making personal sacrifices. This inner conflict between his quiet nature and the need to protect those he loved was something that Charlie worked to portray in a meaningful way. In addition to his emotional preparation, Charlie had to learn the technical aspects of the role. Jonathan was a photographer, so Charlie had to learn to handle a camera and make it look natural.

He practiced his photography skills and learned about capturing moments, which helped him bring a sense of realism to the role. Jonathan's passion for photography was an important part of his character, and Charlie wanted to ensure that it came across clearly in his performance. The chemistry between Charlie and the other cast members was also key to making Jonathan's role work. Jonathan had strong relationships with his friends and family, particularly his brother Will, played by Noah Schnapp. Their bond was one of the emotional cornerstones of the show, and Charlie worked hard to establish a strong connection with Noah. Their scenes were full of emotional depth and helped make Jonathan's character even more compelling. Additionally, Charlie's interactions with other cast members, such as Nancy Wheeler (played by Natalia Dyer), added layers to Jonathan's character, creating a sense of complexity and growth as the story progressed. When Stranger Things premiered, Charlie's performance as Jonathan Byers was praised by fans and critics alike. His portrayal of the quiet, determined, and protective older brother resonated with audiences, and he quickly became a fan favorite. The success of

Stranger Things catapulted Charlie into the spotlight, and his role as Jonathan Byers became the defining moment of his career. He had gone from an aspiring actor to a global star in what seemed like an instant.

How the Show Changed His Life

The debut of Stranger Things in 2016 was a cultural phenomenon. The show's mix of supernatural thrills, heartfelt relationships, and 1980s nostalgia captivated audiences worldwide. This success was life-changing for Charlie Heaton, who played the introspective and protective

Jonathan Byers. Stranger Things didn't just provide him with a platform—it transformed his entire life, professionally and personally, in ways he had never imagined. Before Stranger Things, Charlie was a talented actor trying to make a name for himself in an industry full of challenges. But the show's success brought him instant recognition. Suddenly, he was no longer just another aspiring actor. He was part of a global hit, and his portrayal of Jonathan Byers earned him a dedicated fanbase. People connected with Jonathan's quiet resilience, love for his family, and courage in facing danger. Jonathan was relatable to many viewers, and Charlie's performance made him unforgettable. As Stranger Things gained popularity, so did Charlie. The series opened doors for him that had previously seemed out of reach. Casting directors and filmmakers began to take notice of his talent. Offers for new roles started to come in, and Charlie found himself in a position he had only dreamed of a few years earlier. He was no longer chasing opportunities—they were coming to him. The show's impact on Charlie's personal life was just as profound. Being part of a global sensation meant he was suddenly recognized wherever he went. Fans would stop him on the street to talk about Jonathan, share their love for the show, or ask for a photo. While the attention was overwhelming at times, Charlie appreciated the support and enthusiasm from fans. He understood that Stranger Things wasn't just a show for many people—it was a source of comfort, excitement, and inspiration. However, fame also came with its challenges. Charlie had to adapt to living under the constant scrutiny of the public eye. Every move he made, both on and off the screen, was analyzed and discussed. While he valued his privacy, he recognized that this attention was part of his new reality. Charlie learned to balance his public life with his own, finding ways to stay grounded amidst the whirlwind of fame. One of Charlie's most significant changes was how Stranger Things allowed him to grow as an artist. Working on the show pushed him to hone his craft and explore new depths as an actor. The series demanded intense emotional performances, and Charlie rose to the occasion, delivering powerful and authentic scenes. He worked closely with the show's creators, the Duffer Brothers, to bring Jonathan's character to life, and their collaboration helped him become a more confident and skilled performer. The friendships Charlie formed on set also played a big role in shaping his experience. The cast of Stranger Things became like a second family to him. They supported each other through the ups and downs of fame, celebrating their successes and navigating challenges together. For Charlie, these bonds were invaluable. He often spoke about how much he admired his co-stars and how their camaraderie made working on the show even more special. Stranger Things also allowed Charlie to connect with fans on a deeper level. He often received messages from people who saw themselves in Jonathan Byers—who felt like outsiders, had struggled to protect their families, or had faced challenges in their own lives. These stories touched Charlie, reminding him of the power of storytelling and the impact it could have on people's lives. While the show brought immense joy and opportunities, it also required much hard work. Filming Stranger Things was intense, with long hours on set and emotionally demanding scenes. Charlie embraced these challenges, knowing they were part of creating something special. He poured his heart into every scene, committed to making Jonathan's journey as real and meaningful as possible. The success of Stranger Things also gave Charlie a platform to explore other projects and interests. It allowed him to take on new roles, collaborate with talented filmmakers, and expand his career beyond what he had initially imagined. But despite these new opportunities, Charlie always stayed grounded, remembering the journey that had brought him to this point. Perhaps one of the most profound ways Stranger Things changed Charlie's life was the sense of fulfillment it brought him. Acting had always been his passion, and being part of a show that resonated with so many people made him feel like he was doing something meaningful. It wasn't just about the fame or the recognition—it was about being part of a story that mattered. As Charlie's life evolves after Stranger Things, he never forgets the show's impact. It gave him a chance to shine, grow, and connect with audiences worldwide. For Charlie, Stranger Things wasn't just a chapter in his career—it was a defining moment that shaped who he was as an actor and as a person.

Chapter 5: Life Beyond the Camera

Off-Screen Passions and Projects

Charlie Heaton's life extends beyond the screen's bright lights and high-stakes drama. While his acting career, mainly as Jonathan Byers in Stranger Things, has brought him global fame, there's much more to Charlie than the characters he plays. Away from the camera, he is a profoundly creative and multifaceted individual who pursues his passions and works on personal projects that bring him joy and fulfilment. One of Charlie's most prominent off-screen interests is music. Long before he became an actor, music was his first love. As a teenager growing up in Leeds, he spent hours listening to his favourite bands and experimenting with different sounds. He eventually became a drummer for the band Comanechi, which took him on a whirlwind journey into the music world. Even as his acting career took off, Charlie never let go of his musical roots. For Charlie, music is more than a hobby—it's a way to express himself and stay grounded. Playing the drums or collaborating with other musicians allows him to tap into his creativity differently than acting. He has often spoken about how music provides him a sense of calm and balance, especially during the hectic times. Whenever he has a break from filming, he usually reconnects with his musical side, finding solace in the rhythms and melodies that first inspired him. Beyond music, Charlie has also shown an interest in exploring other art forms. Whether it's photography, painting, or attending art exhibitions, he appreciates the beauty and expression that art brings to the world. His artistic pursuits are a reflection of his curious and reflective nature. He values creativity in all its forms and enjoys learning from other artists and creators. In addition to his artistic passions, Charlie strongly advocates using his platform to have a positive impact. Over the years, he has been involved in various charitable causes and social initiatives. Charlie believes that fame comes with a responsibility to give back, and he takes this responsibility seriously. From raising awareness about mental health to supporting organizations that provide opportunities for young people, Charlie has dedicated time and energy to making a difference in the world. One cause particularly close to his heart is mental health awareness. Having experienced the pressures of fame and the challenges of balancing a demanding career, Charlie understands how important it is to prioritize mental well-being. He has openly shared his struggles, emphasizing the importance of seeking support and breaking down the stigma surrounding mental health issues. By speaking out, he has inspired others to prioritize their mental health and seek help when needed. Another off-screen project that has captured Charlie's attention is his interest in storytelling beyond acting. While he has made a name for himself as an actor, he has expressed a desire to explore writing and directing in the future. Charlie is fascinated by the creative process behind making films and television shows, and he hopes to one day contribute to stories as an actor and storyteller in other capacities. Charlie is also passionate about spending time with his family and close friends. Despite his busy schedule, he prioritizes staying connected to the people who mean the most to him. For Charlie, family is a source of strength and inspiration. His close relationship with his son and his dedication to being a present and supportive parent exemplify how he strives to maintain a healthy work-life balance. Travel is another passion that Charlie cherishes. His career has taken him to many places worldwide, but he also enjoys leisure travel. Exploring new cultures, tasting different cuisines, and meeting people from various walks of life are experiences that fuel his curiosity and broaden his perspective. For Charlie, travel is not just about visiting new places—it's about learning and growing as a person. In recent years, Charlie has also taken an interest in environmental issues. He recognizes the urgency of addressing climate change and has used his voice to promote sustainable living and environmental conservation. Whether it's through supporting eco-friendly initiatives or encouraging his fans to make small changes in their daily lives, Charlie is committed to doing his part to protect the planet. Finally, Charlie values the importance of self-reflection and personal growth. He has spoken about the lessons he has learned throughout his journey as an actor and person. From navigating the highs and lows of fame to discovering new passions, Charlie believes in continually evolving and striving to be his best version. Off-screen, Charlie Heaton is a talented actor and multi-dimensional individual with many interests and passions. Whether making music, exploring art, advocating for important causes, or simply spending time with loved ones, Charlie approaches everything he does with authenticity and enthusiasm. His off-screen life is a testament to his creativity, compassion, and dedication to making the most of every opportunity.

Personal Connections and Relationships

While Charlie Heaton is best known for his work in front of the camera, his personal life has also played a pivotal role in shaping the person he has become. Beyond the glitz and glamour of Hollywood, Charlie's relationships with family, friends, and loved ones around him give him a strong sense of purpose and identity. At the heart of Charlie's personal life is his son, Archie. Becoming a father at a young age was a life-changing experience for Charlie. Although he had just begun to establish himself in the entertainment industry, he embraced fatherhood with an open heart and a solid commitment to being there for his son. Balancing a rising career with parental responsibilities was not always easy. Still, Charlie has spoken about how much Archie means to him and how fatherhood has given him a new perspective on life. His close relationship with

Archie reflects Charlie's desire to stay connected to his roots. No matter how far his career has taken him, he values the importance of family and cherishes the moments he spends with his son. These moments remind him of the importance of love, care, and responsibility, which extend beyond his professional life. In addition to his role as a father, Charlie has also built meaningful relationships within his professional circle. His time on Stranger Things introduced him to an ensemble cast that would become like a second family. His bond with Natalia Dyer, who plays Nancy Wheeler on the show, has been especially significant among them. Their on-screen chemistry as characters quickly blossomed into a real-life relationship. Charlie and Natalia's relationship has captivated fans, but they have always maintained privacy about their personal lives. They prefer to keep the focus on their work, which speaks to their professionalism and shared values. Despite the challenges of navigating a high-profile romance, their connection remains strong, fueled by mutual respect, understanding, and support for each other's careers. Friendships have also played an essential role in Charlie's journey. Charlie has surrounded himself with people who inspire and uplift him. Whether it's childhood friends from Leeds or fellow artists he's met along the way, these relationships serve as a reminder of the power of genuine connection. For Charlie, his friends provide a sense of belonging and stability in an industry that sometimes feels overwhelming. Charlie's relationships extend beyond his personal life, including professional partnerships and collaborations. As a musician, actor, and artist, he values the creative bonds he forms with those he works alongside. These relationships often inspire him to push the boundaries of his craft, exploring new ideas and perspectives that enrich his work. Another vital connection in Charlie's life is with his fans. While fame can sometimes create distance between celebrities and their supporters, Charlie has always made an effort to show his appreciation for those who have supported him throughout his career. He understands his work's impact on people and strives to connect with his audience meaningfully. Whether through social media, interviews, or appearances, Charlie values the opportunity to share his journey and inspire others. The family remains a central theme in Charlie's life. Growing up in Leeds, he was raised in a tight-knit household that taught him the importance of resilience and togetherness. His upbringing shaped his values and continues influencing how he approaches his relationships today. Charlie often reflects on the lessons he learned from his family, which serve as a guiding light in both his personal and professional endeavours. As Charlie's career continues to flourish, he remains mindful of the importance of balance. Maintaining solid personal connections while pursuing his ambitions is no small feat, but he approaches it with the same dedication and determination he brings to his work. For Charlie, these relationships are not just a source of comfort but a cornerstone of his identity and a wellspring of inspiration. His relationships also highlight the importance of vulnerability and authenticity. Charlie's genuine approach to his connections sets him apart in an industry that often prioritizes image over substance. He values honesty and openness, deepening his bonds with the people most matter to him. In many ways, Charlie's connections and relationships mirror the themes of the roles he plays on screen. Like Jonathan Byers, his Stranger Things character, Charlie understands the importance of loyalty, love, and standing by the people you care about. These values resonate in his personal life and artistic endeavours, making him a relatable and inspiring figure.

Chapter 6: Navigating Fame and Challenges

The Pressures of Stardom

For Charlie Heaton, rising to fame brought incredible opportunities and unforeseen challenges. Charlie quickly became a household name as his role on Stranger Things propelled him into the spotlight. However, with great success came the inevitable pressures that accompany life in the public eye. Fame can be thrilling but also demands resilience, focus, and the ability to adapt to a constantly scrutinized life. The journey to stardom is never a straight path. While Charlie was immensely grateful for his success, the sudden shift in his life was sometimes overwhelming. Charlie led a relatively private life before his breakout role as Jonathan Byers. He was free to explore his passions in music and acting without the added weight of public expectation. That freedom drastically changed as the show gained global popularity. One of the most significant pressures of stardom is losing anonymity. For Charlie, navigating a world where fans recognized him wherever he went was both a blessing and a challenge. Fans often approached him with admiration and excitement, which he sincerely appreciated, but constantly being in the public eye meant little room for privacy. Everyday activities, like walking through a park or visiting his favourite coffee shop, suddenly became moments where cameras might follow, and personal space was more challenging to find.The demands of his work only added to the pressure. Being part of a global phenomenon like Stranger Things requires a significant time commitment. Long hours on set, promotional tours, and interviews became his routine. While Charlie enjoyed these aspects of his career, they left little time to rest or spend with his loved ones. Balancing work and personal life became an ongoing struggle that many young stars face as they navigate the entertainment industry. Another challenge Charlie encountered was the pressure to meet the expectations of fans and critics. As an actor, he poured his heart into his roles, striving to bring authenticity to every scene. However, knowing that millions of viewers were watching and judging his performances could be daunting. He wanted to ensure that his work lived up to the high standards of the show's audience while staying true to his artistic vision. Social media amplified these pressures. While platforms like Instagram and Twitter allowed Charlie to connect with fans, they also brought unwanted scrutiny. Thousands of people dissected every post, comment, or public appearance, some of whom offered support and encouragement, while others criticized or speculated about his life. For someone as private as Charlie, managing this level of attention took work. The entertainment industry itself posed its own set of challenges. Hollywood is known for being competitive and fast-paced, with actors constantly vying for roles and relevance. For Charlie, maintaining his career momentum while staying true to his values required careful decision-making. He understood the importance of choosing roles aligned with his passions and avoiding projects that didn't resonate with him. This balance was essential for preserving his authenticity as an artist. Charlie also faced the pressure of maintaining his mental health in such a demanding environment. The high expectations placed on him, combined with the lack of privacy and the intensity of his work, sometimes took a toll on his well-being. To cope, Charlie leaned on his support system, which included family, friends, and colleagues who understood the unique challenges of his career. He also sought solace in his creative outlets, such as music, which provided him with an escape from the stresses of stardom. Despite these challenges, Charlie remained grounded by focusing on what truly mattered. He always remembered why he pursued acting in the first place: his love for storytelling and his desire to connect with audiences. By staying true to his passions and surrounding himself with supportive people, Charlie found ways to navigate the pressures of fame without losing himself. The lessons Charlie learned during this time were invaluable. He discovered the importance of setting boundaries, both personally and professionally. While he cherished his fans, he also recognized the need to carve out moments of privacy to recharge and maintain his sense of self. He learned to prioritize his mental health, understanding that caring for himself was essential for sustaining his career and personal happiness. Charlie's journey highlights the dual nature of fame. While it brought incredible opportunities and opened doors he could only dream of, it also came with challenges that required strength and resilience. His ability to navigate these pressures with grace and authenticity is a testament to his character and determination. Through it all, Charlie remained grateful for the platform his success provided. He used his visibility to support causes he cared about and to inspire others to pursue their dreams, no matter the obstacles. His story serves as a reminder that fame is not just about glitz and glamour; it's about growth, learning, and staying true to oneself in the face of adversity.

Staying Grounded Through It All

Despite the whirlwind of fame that came with his role on Stranger Things, Charlie Heaton managed to stay grounded. Remaining connected to his roots and keeping his priorities in check helped him navigate the pressures of stardom without losing himself. His journey from a small-town dreamer to an internationally recognized actor taught him valuable lessons about humility, self-awareness, and resilience. One of the key factors that kept Charlie grounded was his family. Growing up in Leeds, Charlie was raised in a close-knit household that valued connection and authenticity. Even as his fame grew, he frequently returned home to spend time with his loved ones, ensuring the bond he shared with his family remained strong. His family not only offered a source of comfort and normalcy but also reminded him of where he came from and the values he cherished. Charlie's childhood friends also played an essential role in keeping him grounded. These friendships, built long before the world knew his name, were a source of support and honesty. Unlike many new acquaintances he made in the entertainment world, these friends saw him as Charlie, not a celebrity. They provided a safe space where he could be himself without the expectations or pressures that came with fame. In addition to his relationships, Charlie maintained a solid connection to his passions outside of acting. Music, his first love, remained a creative outlet for him. Although his acting career took centre stage, Charlie never stopped his passion for drumming and performing. Music allowed him to express himself in a way that was free from the scrutiny of the public eye, providing a sense of freedom and grounding amidst the chaos of his acting career. Nature also became a source of solace for Charlie. Whenever he could, he sought out quiet moments away from the spotlight, often escaping to peaceful, secluded places where he could reflect and recharge. These moments of stillness helped him maintain balance and clarity, reminding him of the simple joys in life that fame could never replace. Charlie's approach to fame was also shaped by his ability to set boundaries. While he was grateful for his fans and the opportunities his success provided, he recognized the importance of protecting his personal life. He learned to say no to specific engagements and to prioritize his mental health and well-being. Setting these boundaries allowed him to stay true to himself and avoid becoming overwhelmed by the demands of his career. In interviews, Charlie often spoke about his gratitude for the opportunities he'd been given. He acknowledged the privilege of being part of a groundbreaking show like Stranger Things and its impact on his life. However, he was also candid about the challenges of fame, using his platform to encourage others to focus on what truly matters—family, passion, and self-care. Another way Charlie stayed grounded was by giving back. He used his growing platform to support causes that were meaningful to him, such as mental health awareness and environmental conservation. Engaging in charitable efforts reminded him of the power of using his fame for good, allowing him to connect with others meaningfully beyond the entertainment industry. Charlie's humility also played a significant role in his ability to navigate fame. Despite his success, he remained approachable and down-to-earth. Colleagues on set described him as kind, collaborative, and deeply committed to his craft. His grounded attitude earned him respect from his peers and fans, proving that fame doesn't have to change a person's core values. Charlie also developed a deeper understanding of himself as he grew more accustomed to life in the spotlight. His challenges taught him resilience, patience, and the importance of staying true to his passions. He realized that fame was just one aspect of his journey and that the most meaningful parts of his life were the connections he built and his impact on others. Through it all, Charlie's authenticity shone brightly. He remained focused on what mattered most to him—his family, friends, and love for storytelling. He continued to pursue roles that resonated with him, prioritizing quality over quantity in his career choices. He maintained his integrity by staying true to himself and inspiring others to do the same. Charlie Heaton's story is a powerful example of how staying grounded can help one navigate the complexities of fame. His ability to balance the demands of stardom with his values is a testament to his strength of character. For

Charlie, fame was never about glitz and glamour; it was about using his platform to inspire, connect, and remain faithful to the dreams that first set him on this incredible journey.

Chapter 7: Looking Ahead: The Future of Charlie Heaton

Dreams Beyond Acting

As Charlie Heaton's acting career continues to thrive, he remains someone who dreams beyond the confines of a single profession. While his role as Jonathan Byers in Stranger Things cemented his place in the entertainment industry, Charlie's aspirations extend far beyond acting. A man of many talents, he envisions a future filled with creative exploration, meaningful projects, and personal growth. One of Charlie's deepest passions has always been music. Before stepping into the acting world, Charlie's heart was set on drumming, a craft he perfected during his time with the band Comanechi. Music allowed him to express himself in ways that words could not. Even as acting became his primary focus, the rhythm of drums and melodies of music remained an essential part of his life. Charlie often speaks about his dream to revisit his musical roots, possibly creating or collaborating on projects that merge his acting career with his musical background. For Charlie, music is not just a pastime—it is an outlet for storytelling, much like acting. He dreams of composing music for films or even performing on stage again. These ambitions reflect his desire to combine his two great loves into one creative venture. Whether behind the drum kit or lending his voice to a soundtrack, Charlie's future in music promises to be as dynamic and fulfilling as his acting career. Another dream of Charlie's lies in directing and producing. After years of working in front of the camera, he has developed a deep appreciation for the artistry and collaboration required to bring a story to life. He often talks about the directors he has worked with, admiring their vision and leadership. Inspired by their work, Charlie envisions stepping into this role one day, crafting stories from behind the scenes. For Charlie, directing is not just about technical expertise but guiding a narrative and helping actors unlock their best performances. He dreams of telling unique stories that resonate with audiences personally. Whether it's a thought-provoking indie film or a gripping drama, Charlie's passion for storytelling ensures that his contributions as a director would be as heartfelt as his performances on screen. Beyond the entertainment industry, Charlie is equally committed to using his platform for good. As someone who understands the pressures and challenges of fame, he has become an advocate for mental health awareness. He dreams of supporting initiatives that provide resources and support to those struggling with mental well-being. Charlie believes in the power of open conversations and hopes to contribute to destigmatizing mental health issues, especially among young people. In addition to mental health advocacy, Charlie is passionate about environmental conservation. Having grown up in the countryside of Leeds, he feels a deep connection to nature and recognizes the urgent need to protect it. He dreams of collaborating with organizations that promote sustainability by raising awareness, funding research, or participating in campaigns. For Charlie, giving back to the planet ensures that future generations can enjoy the beauty of the natural world. As Charlie looks ahead, he also dreams of exploring roles that challenge him in new ways. While his work on Stranger Things has been transformative, he knows there is still much to learn and accomplish. He hopes to take on characters that push him out of his comfort zone, exploring different genres and styles of storytelling. From historical dramas to futuristic sci-fi, Charlie's versatility as an actor makes these ambitions well within his reach. Despite his lofty dreams, Charlie remains focused on personal growth and happiness. He dreams of balancing his professional aspirations with a fulfilling personal life. His priorities are spending time with family, maintaining close friendships, and nurturing his relationships. He often talks about the importance of staying connected to the people who matter most, even as his career takes him to new heights. Travel is another dream that Charlie holds dear. As someone who has already experienced the thrill of performing and acting on an international stage, he hopes to continue exploring the world. Whether discovering new cultures, trying different cuisines, or simply taking in the beauty of unfamiliar landscapes, Charlie sees travel as a way to enrich his life and inspire his creative pursuits. Ultimately, Charlie Heaton's dreams are a reflection of his multifaceted personality. He is an artist, a storyteller, and a dreamer who refuses to be defined by a single label. His aspirations remind us that pursuing multiple passions is possible while staying true to oneself. Whether acting, making music, directing, or giving back to the community, Charlie's journey is one of growth, exploration, and unwavering commitment to his craft.

What's Next for a Rising Star

As Charlie Heaton continues to rise in the entertainment world, one question lingers: what's next for this multi-talented artist? After making his mark as Jonathan Byers in Stranger Things, Charlie has proven his ability to captivate audiences. But for him, success is not just about staying in the spotlight—it's about evolving as an artist and exploring new horizons. Charlie's career has been a testament to his versatility and determination. He has transitioned from a small-town musician in Leeds to a globally recognized actor. With the final season of Stranger Things on the horizon, fans are eager to see what he will tackle next. Charlie's future, however, is not confined to one path; it is a mix of dreams, ambitions, and the willingness to take risks. One of Charlie's next steps is diving into more challenging and diverse acting roles. Having built his career on playing a complex, reflective character, he now seeks opportunities to showcase his range. Whether it's a fast-paced action thriller, an emotional drama, or an offbeat independent film, Charlie is excited about exploring new genres. He believes that stepping out of his comfort zone is the key to growth, and he's eager to take on characters that challenge him unexpectedly. Beyond acting, Charlie is also looking to expand his creative contributions behind the scenes. The idea of directing or producing intrigues him, and he dreams of telling stories that resonate deeply with audiences. Having observed talented directors throughout his career, Charlie is inspired to bring his vision to life. He hopes to work on projects that allow him to collaborate with diverse voices and ensure his stories reflect various perspectives. Charlie's love for music is another area he wants to revisit. While his acting career has taken centre stage recently, music remains a core part of his identity. He dreams of returning to the studio or even performing live again. Whether it's as a drummer, songwriter, or collaborator, Charlie envisions a future where music and acting coexist in harmony. He says music offers a unique way to connect with people, and he hopes to use it as another medium to tell meaningful stories. In addition to his creative pursuits, Charlie is deeply committed to making a difference in the world. He understands the power of his platform and aims to use it responsibly. Mental health advocacy is one cause that resonates strongly with him. Having faced personal struggles and the pressures of fame, Charlie wants to support others going through similar challenges. He dreams of partnering with organizations that provide mental health resources, particularly for young people navigating difficult times. Environmental conservation is another passion close to Charlie's heart. Growing up surrounded by the natural beauty of Leeds, he developed a deep appreciation for the environment. He hopes to work with initiatives that promote sustainability and protect the planet. Whether through public campaigns or behind-the-scenes efforts, Charlie is determined to contribute to a cause that ensures a brighter future for future generations.On a personal level, Charlie values balance and connection. As his career grows, he remains focused on nurturing relationships and staying grounded. Spending time with his family, close friends, and loved ones is his priority. He believes true success is about professional achievements and maintaining meaningful connections with the people who matter most. Travel is another exciting chapter in Charlie's future. Having already experienced the thrill of performing and acting on an international stage, he hopes to continue exploring the world. Travel inspires him, broadens his perspective, and fuels his creativity. Whether exploring new cultures, finding inspiration for a role, or simply enjoying the beauty of a distant land, travel is an essential part of his journey. As Charlie looks ahead, he is also mindful of leaving a lasting legacy. He dreams of being remembered as a talented actor or musician and someone who inspired others to follow their passions. He hopes his journey—from a small-town dreamer in Leeds to a global star—encourages others to believe in themselves and take risks, no matter how daunting the path may seem. Charlie Heaton's bright future is filled with endless and untapped possibilities. Whether he's taking on bold new roles, creating music, advocating for important causes, or simply living life to the fullest, one thing is sure:

he will continue to surprise and inspire. For Charlie, the journey is just as important as the destination, and he's excited to see where the next chapter takes him.

Conclusion

One thing becomes crystal clear as we reach the end of Charlie Heaton's incredible story: his journey is a testament to perseverance, talent, and the courage to dream big. From humble beginnings in Leeds to becoming an internationally recognized actor, Charlie's path was never straightforward. But the challenges he faced, the risks he took, and the passion he poured into his craft make his story truly inspiring. Reflecting on Charlie's journey, we see a young boy from a small town who dared to dream beyond the world he knew. His love for music led him to explore his creative side, and his journey as a drummer shaped his understanding of hard work and discipline. When acting came into his life, Charlie didn't hesitate to embrace the unknown. Instead, he put his heart and soul into learning, evolving, and growing as an artist. What stands out about Charlie's story is his ability to stay true to himself despite the pressures of fame. In the glitz and glamour of Hollywood, Charlie remains grounded, connected to his roots, and focused on what truly matters—his art, his family, and his values. His humility, dedication, and passion for storytelling serve as a reminder that success is not just about the destination but about the journey and the impact we leave along the way. Charlie's rise to fame with Stranger Things catapulted him into the spotlight and gave him a platform to inspire others. His portrayal of Jonathan Byers—a loyal, thoughtful, and courageous character—resonated with millions of viewers worldwide. But beyond his on-screen success, Charlie's off-screen authenticity and openness about his struggles remind us that everyone faces challenges no matter how successful. His honesty encourages others to embrace their vulnerabilities and seek strength in their passions. The legacy Charlie Heaton is building goes beyond his acting roles or music achievements. It's about the example he sets for aspiring artists and dreamers everywhere. Charlie's story teaches us that no dream is too big and no obstacle too great if we're willing to work hard, believe in ourselves, and stay true to who we are. His journey shows that even when the odds seem stacked against us, there's always a way forward if we persevere. Charlie's ability to evolve—whether through his transition from music to acting or his exploration of new roles—demonstrates the power of adaptability. Life often throws unexpected opportunities, and Charlie's story encourages us to embrace them openly. By stepping out of his comfort zone, he discovered new passions and talents that have shaped the artist he is today. Let Charlie Heaton's journey be a beacon of hope and encouragement for anyone reading this biography. Whether you're pursuing a creative dream, facing challenges, or searching for your purpose, Charlie's story reminds us that success combines passion, persistence, and a willingness to take risks. It's about finding what makes you come alive and dedicating yourself to it, even when the path ahead seems uncertain. Charlie's legacy is also about using his platform to make a positive difference. From his advocacy for mental health awareness to his commitment to staying authentic, Charlie shows that true success isn't just about personal achievement—it's about lifting others and inspiring them to be their best selves. His journey is a powerful reminder that we all have the potential to leave a meaningful impact on the world. As we close the final chapter of this biography, it's important to remember that Charlie Heaton's story is far from over. With his talent, passion, and drive, there's no doubt that the future holds even more extraordinary accomplishments for him. But perhaps the most inspiring part of his journey is not what he's achieved so far but how he's achieved it—with humility, determination, and an unwavering belief in his dreams. To the reader, take this story as a source of motivation. Let Charlie's journey encourage you to dream big, work hard, and never give up. Whether your passion lies in the arts, sciences, sports, or anything else, remember that the road to success is paved with perseverance and a willingness to keep moving forward, even when difficult. Charlie Heaton's legacy is still unfolding, but one thing is sure: he's shown us that no matter where you come from, no matter the challenges you face, you can create a life that is meaningful, impactful, and true to who you are. His story celebrates resilience, creativity, and the power of following your heart. So, as you close this book, take the lessons of Charlie's life with you. Let them remind you that anything is possible when you believe in yourself. Charlie Heaton's journey proves that the stars are within reach—if only you dare to chase them.

www.ingramcontent.com/pod-product-compliance
Lightning Source LLC
Chambersburg PA
CBHW071031240526
45469CB00006BD/2168